I Can Read Chinese

CW01662793

Why?

This book is the first of a series in which we use pictures to show the origins of the basic symbols. It is the key to learning Chinese characters.

Chinese writing consisted of pictures that later became symbols. There is no alphabet. If you learn the pictures, you can recognise the symbols and understand the meaning.

'Radicals' are basic symbols. They can be words in themselves, or only part of a word. For example, the radical 'plant' (木) is a word but also a component of the characters for 'fruit' (果),'tea' (茶), 'vegetable' (菜) etc.

If you learn these basic symbols, it is helpful for you in recognising other symbols which are made up from them. For example, any character containing the 'person' radical will be to do with 'humans'. In the following text, symbols which are radicals are shown by (R) if they can stand alone, and (R+) if they need to be combined with other elements.

Chinese characters are formed in six ways:
1. A picture. E.g. sun, moon. *(see p28, 30)*
2. A symbol (sometimes a picture modified with short or long strokes). E.g. 'sun' plus two strokes indicating the sun rising

over the horizon and the meaning is 'early' or 'morning'. *(see p32)*

3. Combining two or more of the same or different characters (for their meanings). E.g. 'sun' and 'moon' make 'bright'. Or, three 'plants' make 'forest'. *(see p87, 88)*
4. As 3 (but using one for its sound). E.g. 'person' [rén] with 'doors' [mén] (more than one door) means 'persons' [mén] (more than one person). *(see p86)*
5. Other (similar) meaning(s) for an existing character. E.g. 'bell' - also used for 'leader'. (Normally the leader will ring the bell at the front of the procession).
6. Characters can be formed as in 5 above but with different meanings, usually for abstract ideas. An example is the symbol for 'snake', which is used for the symbol 'it', because snakes were the most frequently seen creatures in China.

If it seems that a Chinese character no longer resembles the original idea, it is because it has been drawn for thousands of years and has gradually changed to make it easier to draw.

As the English have Pitman's shorthand system, the Chinese have one mainly based on simplified versions of the original characters. Unfortunately, many have been simplified so much that they have to be learnt separately, some are still recognisable and others have remained the same. Therefore, in this book, we use the full form of the Chinese characters.

In chinese, 'bà' and 'bà bȧ' both mean father, but 'bà' is a word of one syllable and 'bà bȧ' is two words of one syllable each. This is because the Chinese regard every syllable as a word.

Although Chinese words consist only of one syllable, in speech and modern writing another syllable, i.e. another word, is added to make sure the correct meaning has been received. For example, [dòu] is beans and [péng] is friend, but Chinese would normally say [dòu zi] and [péng yǒu]. Most of the extra syllables mean rather the same- e.g. [péng yǒu] literally means 'friend friend'.

In English, 'Book' plus 'End' says 'Bookend', whereas in Chinese 'book' plus 'end' does not say 'bookend' - they will become one syllable, and probably sound quite different and mean quite different.

For instance, the word for 'bright' is written combining the symbols for 'sun' (日) which has the sound [rì] and 'moon' (月) which has the sound [yuè], but it is not pronounced [rìyuè], it is pronounced [míng] (明), another sound altogether. If the symbols are separate they say (日) [rì] and (月) [yuè].

Therefore, even if you learn to read Chinese, you may not know its sound. Methods have been developed to help you, and the most common method is known as 'Pinyin', which means to 'spell the sound'.

The idea is to use English letters to represent Chinese sounds as closely as possible. In this series, we use Pinyin to give the sound. Some words are followed by a '[ ]' containing English letters which are 'Pinyin' for that word.

Most letters in Pinyin are read as in English, but some of them need examples:
c = *ts* in *cats*
q = *ch* in *cheese*
x = *sh* in *ship*
z = *ds* in *kids*
zh = *j* in *jug*

There are also five signs to tell you the tone of the word:
¯ = high (no falling or rising)
ˊ = rising
ˇ = falling-rising
ˋ = falling
· = very short

At the end of each book, we include examples of compound symbols, made from the basic symbols, and how they are used.

我會讀中國字

第一集

為什麼?

這是一系列書的第一本.是用圖畫來介紹基本的中國字根.學會了這些字根,就好像拿到了中國文字寶庫的鑰匙.

中國文字是從圖畫演變來的.它沒有字母.如果你學會認識這些圖畫,你就能認識這些字和它們的意思.

有些基本的中國字是字根.有的字根是一個字,有的字根只是字的一部分.例如,'木'這個字根是一個字,也是'果','茶','菜'等等這些字的一部分.

學會這些基本字根,可以幫助你認識那些由它們組成的中國字.例如,有'人'作為字的一部分時,都是用來表示和人有關的觀念.在這本書裏面,(R)這個記號是指那些是字的字根,而(R+)是指那些不是字的字根.

中國文字有六種形成的方式:

1. 象形:例如'日''月'.
2. 指示:用符號表示意思.(有時候是圖象上加上或長或短的筆劃).例如,'早'是在'日'字加上兩筆,象徵著太陽從地平線升起.表示太陽剛出來的時候,時間上比較前面的意思.
3. 會意:兩個或兩個以上相同或不同的文字結合,形成新的意思.例如,'日'和'月'組合成'明'.或三個'木'組合成

‘森’.

4. 形聲:與 3 相似, 但是取用其中一部分的讀音.例如, ‘人’[rén]和‘們’[mén]組合成‘們’[mén].

5. 轉注:給已經有的文字一個新的, 相似的意思.例如, ‘令’也用作‘領導’的意思.(通常領導的人會用鈴聲來引導人們).

6. 假借:形成方式和 5 相似,但給已有的文字不相同的意思.通常是抽象的.例如,‘它’原本是‘蛇’的意思.因為在中國,蛇是最常見的動物,所以用來表示所有的‘它’.

你可能會覺得有些字和它的圖象不太相像, 那是因為從圖畫變成文字已經很久了, 再加上為了書寫方便, 於是慢慢地改變了.

就像英文有簡筆的速記寫法, 中國文字也有把繁體簡化的簡體.但是許多字被簡化得太多, 以至於不能從字形認出它的意思.有些簡體字還可以看出它原來的圖象, 但更有些字沒有被簡化.所以, 這本書選用了繁體字.

在中文裏,‘爸’和‘爸爸’的意思是一樣的.不過,‘爸’是一個音節,一個字.而‘爸爸’是兩個單音節的詞.事實上,每個中國字只有一個音節.

雖然每個中國字只有一個音節, 在說話或寫白話文的時候, 為了要說清楚一些, 常常要加上另一個音節(也就是另一個字).例如, ‘豆’和‘朋’通常要說成‘豆子’和‘朋友’.這個加上去的字, 大部分是和原來那個字的意思一樣, 例如‘朋友’, 其實和‘朋’或‘友’是一樣的.

在英文裏, ‘書’加上‘末’, 通常就唸作‘書末’.在中文裏, 如果有個字是‘書’加上‘末’, 它並不會唸作‘書末’, 而是變成一個音節的字. 有時候是一個和‘書’或‘末’完全不相同的音.
例如, ‘明’這個字是由‘日’和‘月’兩個字組成的, 可是它不唸作‘日月’, 而唸作‘明’和‘日月’完全不同.如果‘日’‘月’分成兩個字來寫, 他們就分別唸作‘日’‘月’.

所以, 就算你會認中國字, 你可不一定能唸得出來那個字.有些人想了辦法來幫助人們唸中國字.在這些辦法中, 拼音是最常用的. 它是用英文字母來表示中國字的讀音.雖然不能十分準確, 但是已經很接近了.在這一系列的書裏, 我們選用了拼音.書裏有些字的後面, 用‘[ ]’這個符號包起來的英文字母, 就是那個字的拼音.

大部分拼音的讀法和英文一樣,不過有些讀音需要舉例來說明:

c = ca*ts* 的 *ts*
q = *ch*eese 的 *ch*
x = *sh*ip 的 *sh*
z = ki*ds* 的 *ds*
zh = *j*ug 的 *j*

除了拼音以外,還有五種發聲符號,告訴你這個字的聲調是什麼:

¯ = 一聲（平聲沒有提高或降低）

／= 二聲（由低而高）

∨= 三聲（先降低再提高）

╲ = 四聲（由高而低）

· = 輕聲（非常短）

在這一系列的每一本書的最後面, 我們都示範一些由書裏介紹過的字根組成的字, 和一些由他們組成的詞語.

A man =人[rén]= person, used as part of signs to do with persons (R) (The combining form is mostly '亻 ').

人

丿 人

一個人 =人 [rén] =人.作為字的一部分時表示和人有關的觀念(多半寫作‘亻’).

A man with arms and legs outstretched to exaggerate his size = 大[dà] = big, large, great (R).

大

一 ナ 大

人伸開手腳來表示尺寸很大 =大[dà] =不小

A woman with arms folded = 女[nǚ] = woman (R).

女

兩隻手臂交叉坐著的女人 = 女[nǚ] = 女的

A baby with arms outstretched = 子 [zǐ] = baby; child (R); often added to words to make them clearer.

子

乛 了 子

兩隻手臂伸開的嬰孩＝ 子[zǐ] ＝小孩兒;也常常用作詞尾,使說的話清楚些.

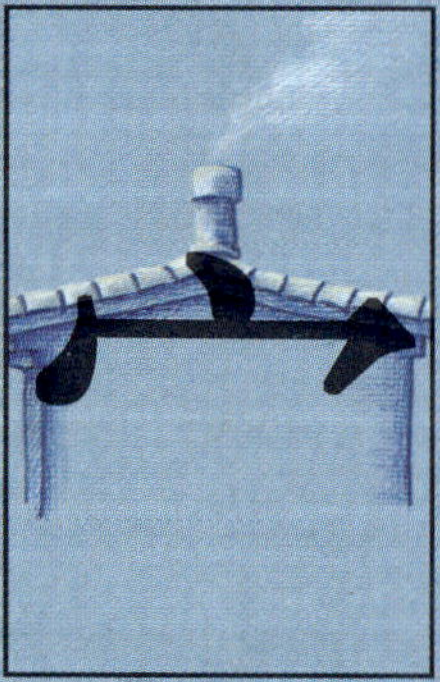

A roof with a chimney = 宀 [mián] = used as part of signs to do with house and home, e.g. home, room (R+).

有煙囪的屋頂 = 宀[mián] = 和房子有關的字根.例如:家,室.

A growing plant = 生 [shēng]= birth, to be born, growth, growing, raw (R).

生

長著嫩芽的植物 = 生[shēng] = 出生;生長;不熟的.

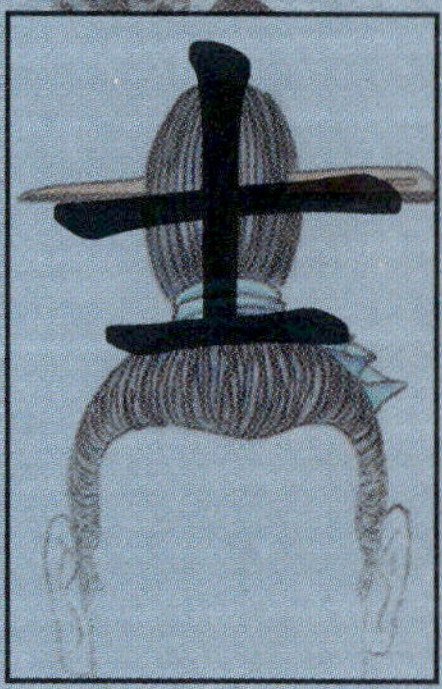

A traditional Chinese scholar's hair style (with a large hairpin) = 士[shì] = scholar (R).

士

一 十 士

傳統中國讀書人的髮型(插著長髮簪) = 士[shì] = 讀書人

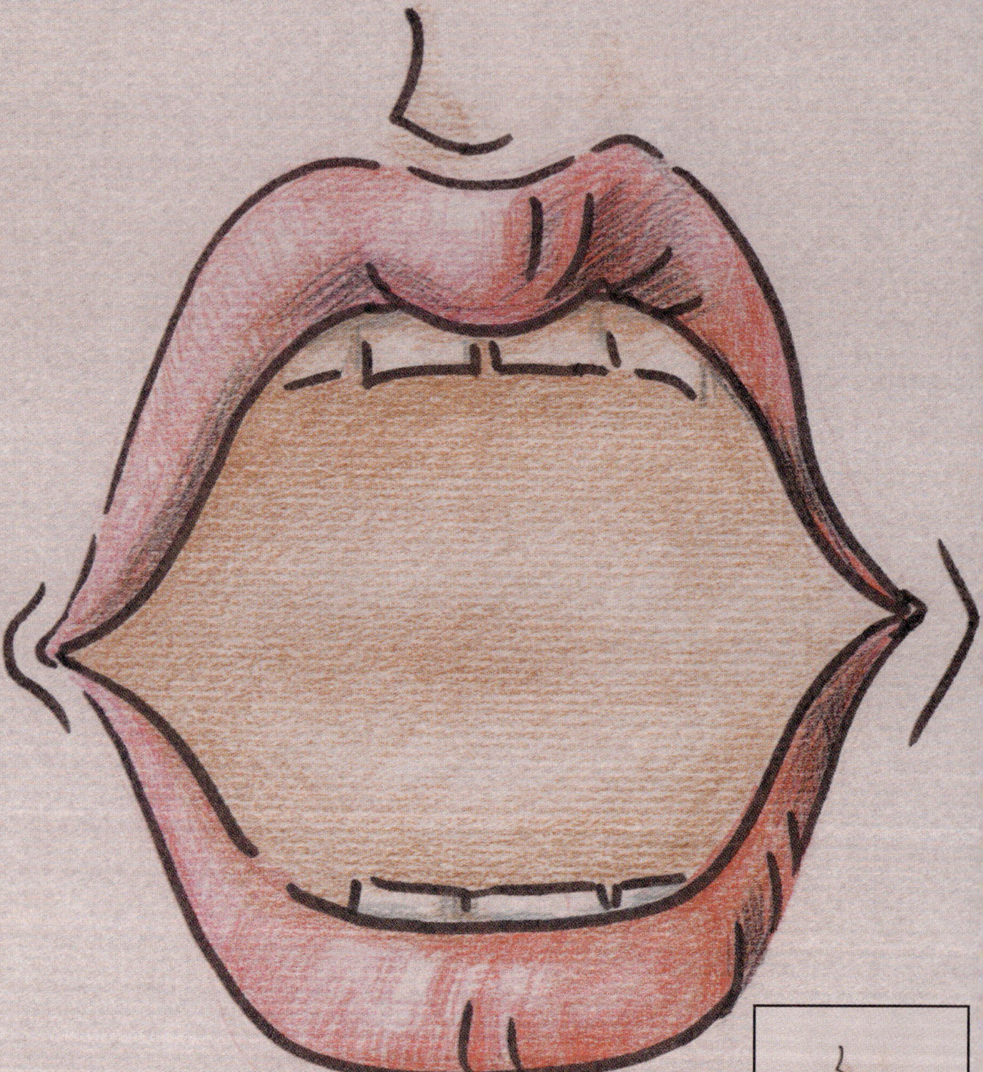

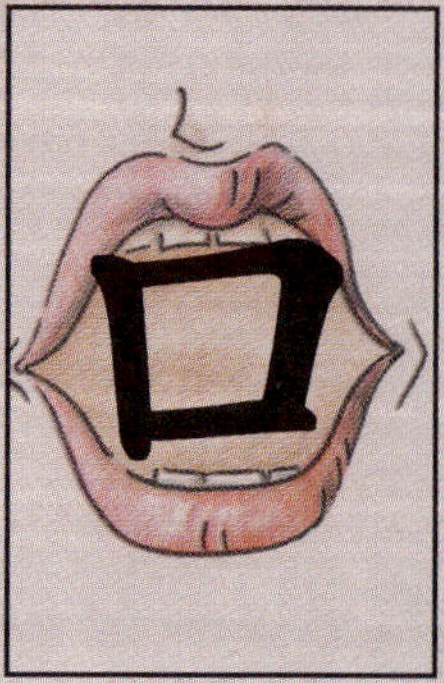

An open mouth = 口 [kǒu] = mouth (R).

口

丨 冂 口

張開的嘴 = 口[kǒu] = 嘴;進出的通道.

A pair of panelled doors = 門[mén]= door (R).

門

一對雙扇門 = 門[mén] = 進出的地方

A pair of panelled doors and a pair of hands withdrawing two bolts = 開[kāi] to open, to operate.

開

一雙手正在移開雙扇門的門閂 = 開[kāi] =打開

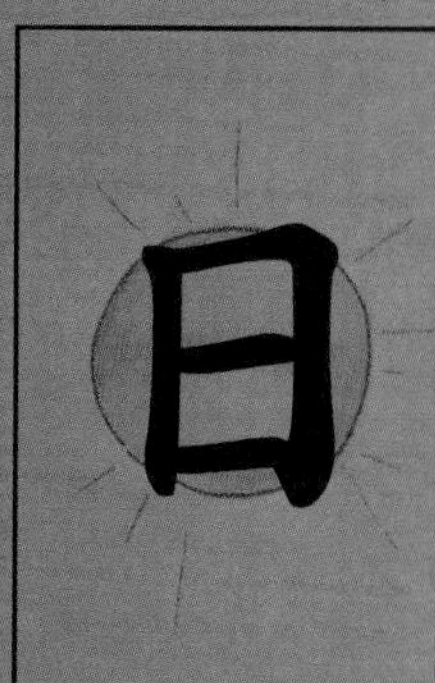

A sun (the inside stroke indicating the sun is solid) = 日 [rì] = sun, day (R).

日

太陽(中間的一畫表示太陽是實心的) =日[rì] =太陽;日子.

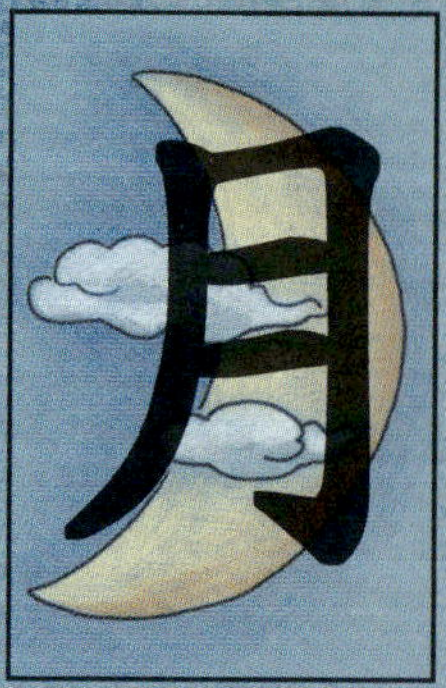

A crescent (the strokes inside indicating the moon is solid). A full moon would be confused with the sun) = 月 [yuè]= moon, month (R).

月

丿 ⺆ 月 月

弦月(中間的一畫表示月亮是實心的).(如果畫滿月就會和'太陽'分不清了) =月[yùe] =月亮;月(計算時間的單位).

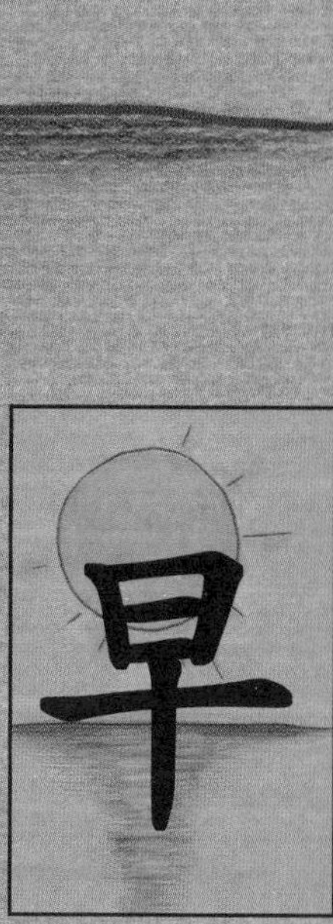

Sun rising above the horizon = 早[zǎo] = morning, early.

早

太陽從地平線升起 = 早[zǎo] = 太陽剛出來的時候;時間上比較前面的.

The sun is high in the sky and too bright to see the shape = 午[wǔ] = midday.

午

太陽高高掛在天空上,而且太明亮了,所以看不清楚它的形狀 = 午[wǔ] =白天 11 點 - 1 點的時間.

A partly seen crescent moon - the sky not completely dark - hence the beginning of the night (dusk or evening) = 夕[xì] = dusk; evening (literary use) (R).

夕

ノ ク 夕

只看到一部分的弦月-因為天空還沒有完全變黑.用剛出來的月亮表示晚上的開始(黃昏) =夕[xì] (屬於文學的用法) = 黃昏

Simplified arrow rising from a ground line
= 上 [shàng] = up.

上

丨 ⺊ 上

向上指的箭頭 ＝ 上[shàng] ＝ 向上

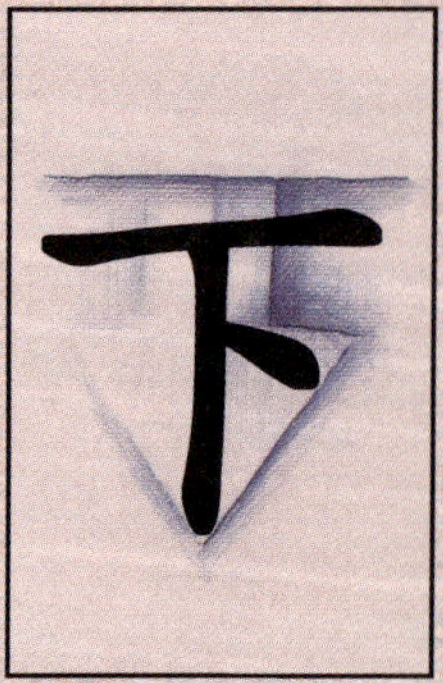

The ‘up’ sign upside-down and slightly changed =下[xìa]= down.

向下指的箭頭 ＝ 下[xìa]＝ 向下

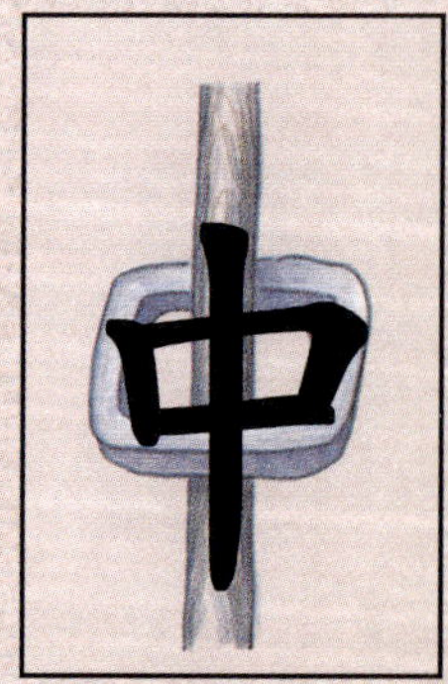

A pole through the middle of a ring. Indicating the centre = 中 [zhōng] = middle, centre.

中

丨 冂 口 中

一根木棍穿過一個環形的中間 = 中[zhōng] = 中間;中心.

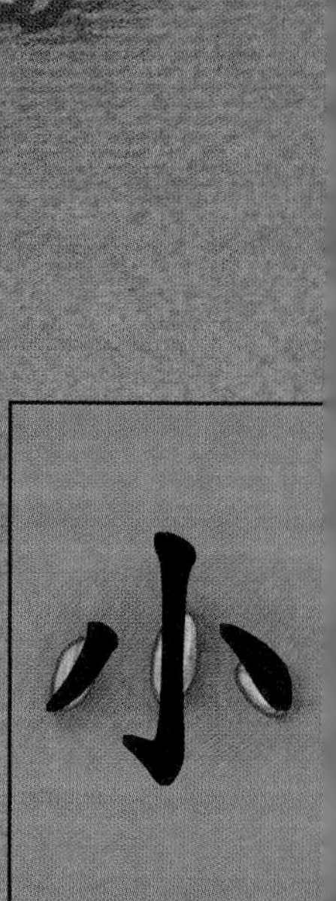

Three grains (One grain would not be distinctive enough) = 小 [xiǎo] = small; tiny (R).

小

三粒穀米 (如果只畫一粒穀米不能夠表示清楚) ＝ 小[xiǎo] ＝ 不大

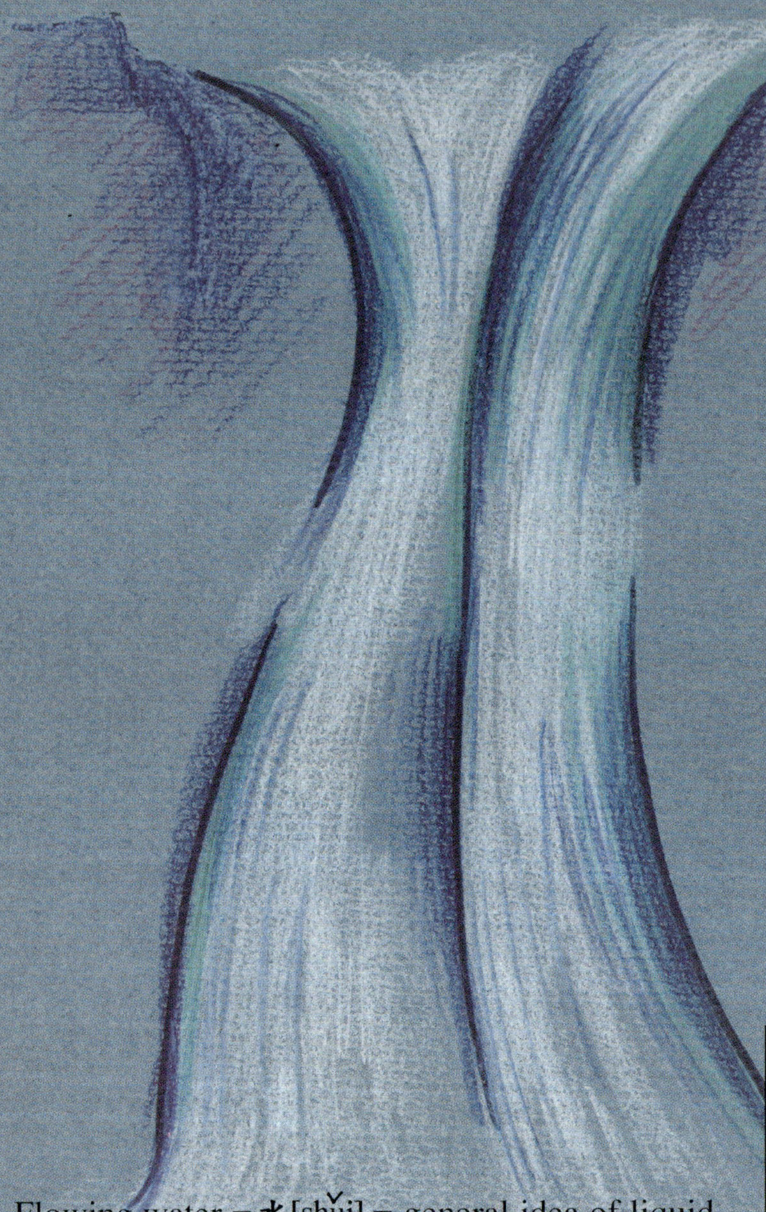

Flowing water = 水[shǔi] = general idea of liquid including water (R). When with other symbols, this symbol normally becomes (氵) - three splashes.

水

流動的水 = 水[shuǐ] = 和液體有關的(包括水).作為字的一部分時,大多寫成(氵) - 三點水花.

Flames rising from burning wood = 火[huǒ] = fire (R). When combine with other symbols sometimes becomes (灬).

火

火焰從一堆燃料中升起 = 火[hǔo] = 燃燒時產生的光和熱.
作為字的一部分時有時寫成(灬).

Two young shoots = 艸 or 艹 [cǎo] = (with other symbols) meaning flowers, leaves, grass, shoots, buds (R+).

兩株嫩芽 = 艸 物艹 [cǎo] = 和花,葉,草,芽,苞有關的字根.

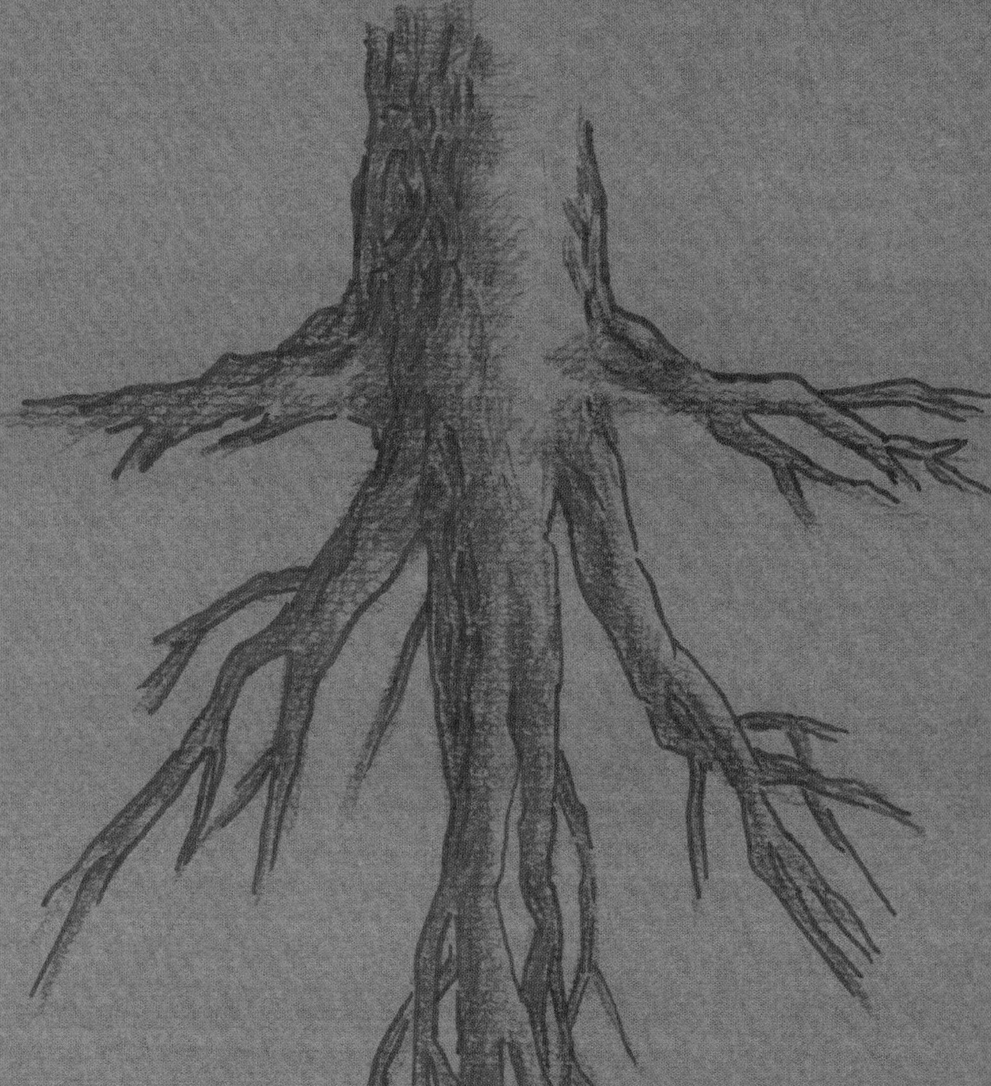

A tree stump with strong roots = 木[mù]= means tree, shrub, bushes and plants; wood (the material) (R).

木

一 十 才 木

樹幹和強韌的根 = 木[mù] = 這字根用來指樹,矮樹叢,灌木,這些和植物或木材有關的東西.

Some fruits growing on a tree = 果[gǔo] = which with other characters can mean fruit, nut (R).

果

丨 冂 冃 日 旦 甲

果 果

長著果子的樹 ＝ 果[gǔo] ＝ 長在植物上的果子. 加上別的字可以指'水果','乾果'.

Two hands picking leaves from a tea plant =茶[chá] = tea.

茶

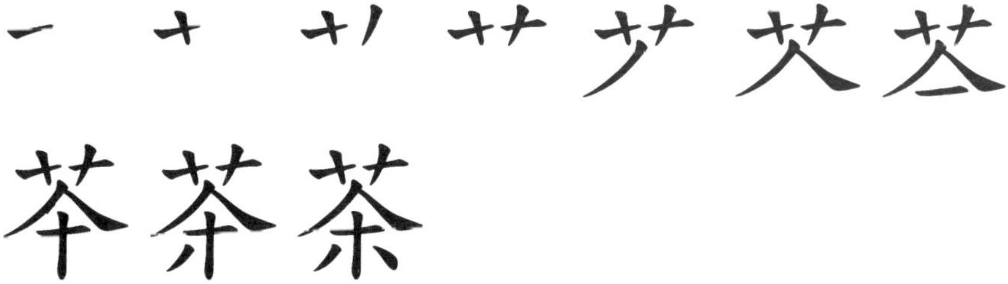

兩隻手摘著茶葉 = 茶[chá] = 一種飲料

A hand pulling a vegetable = 菜[cài] = vegetable.

菜

一隻手拔著蔬菜 ＝ 菜[cài]＝ 蔬菜

A cereal plant = 禾[hé] = crop (R).

禾

一株穀禾 = **禾**[hé] = **穀禾**

Sickle - representing harvesting each year
= 年[nián] = year.

年

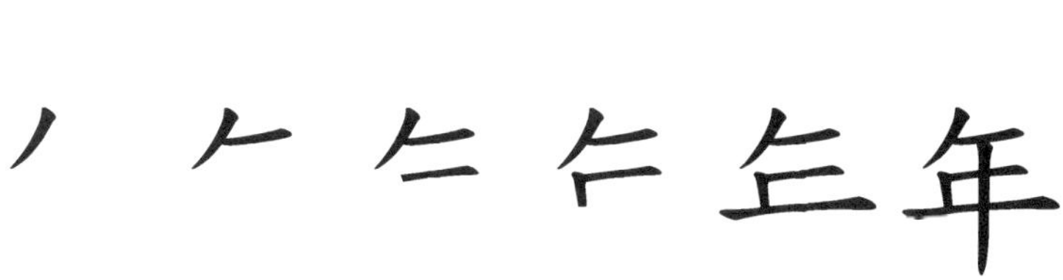

用鐮刀收割-表示一年一次的收穫 ＝ 年[nián] = 365 天

A food plant (People come to obtain food)
= 來 [lái] = come.

來

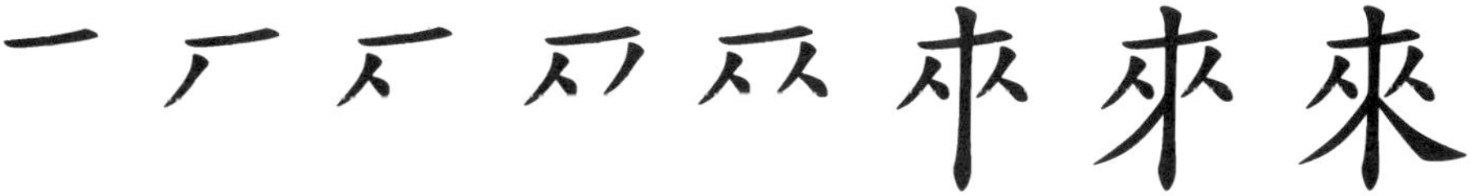

長著食物的植物 (人們來摘取食物) = 來[lái] = 來到

A person leaving a house and stepping over a raised doorstep = 去[qù] = to go.

去

一 十 土 去 去

人跨過門檻出門 = 去[qù] = 離開

Originally a circular ripple of water - but has become rectangular = 回 [huí] = return.

回

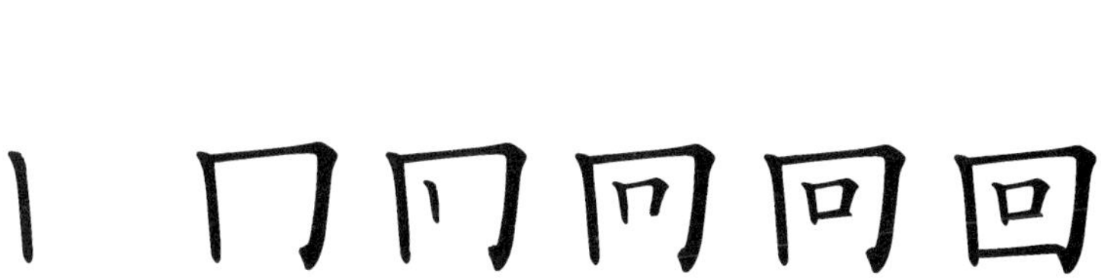

回轉的圓形水漩渦 - 後來寫成方形的 ＝ 回[húi]＝回來

Plan of four fields = 田 [tián] = field(s) (R).

田

四塊相連的田地 ＝ 田[tián]＝ 可以種植的地

Upper arm and forearm using a hoe = 力 [lì]
= strength; power (R).

力

𠃌 力

用手臂操作鋤頭 = 力[lì] = 力量

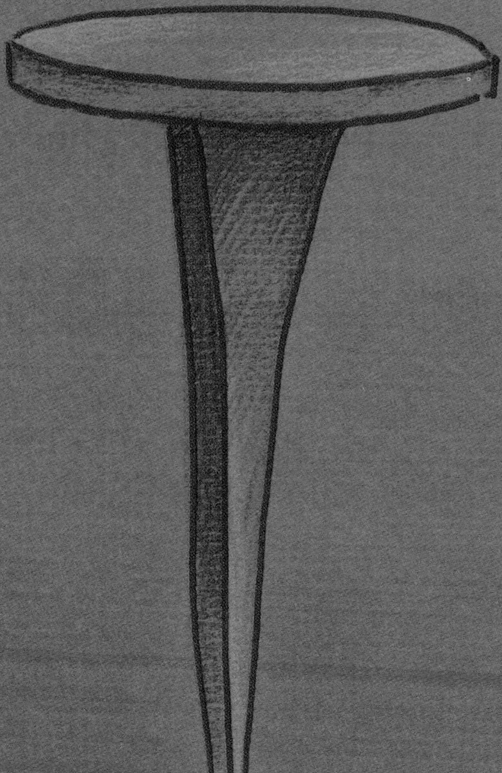

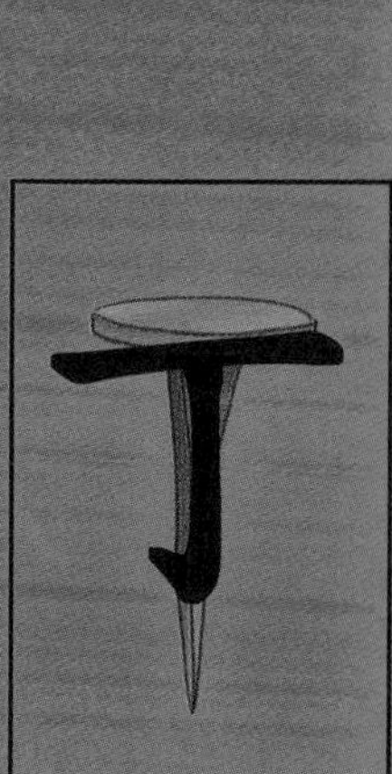

A nail (suggesting firmly fixed and consequently a strong person = 丁 [dīng] = cubic; physically strong person.

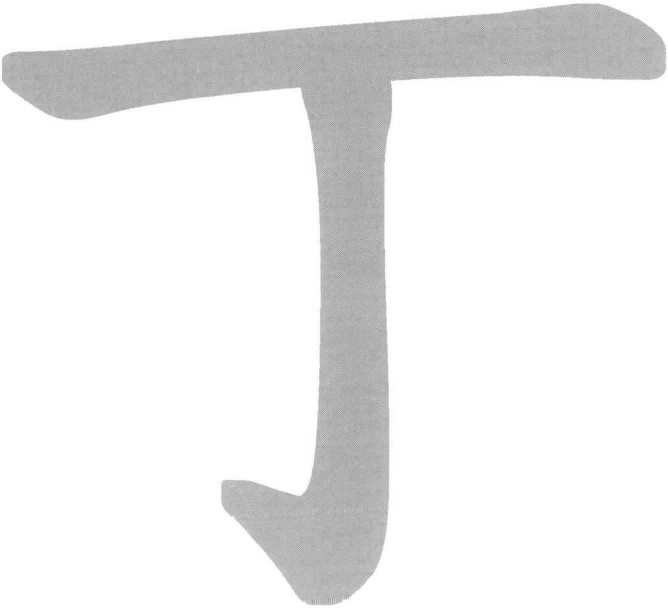

釘子(有固定的意思,因此有強壯的意思) = 丁[dīng] = 小立方體,身體強壯的人.

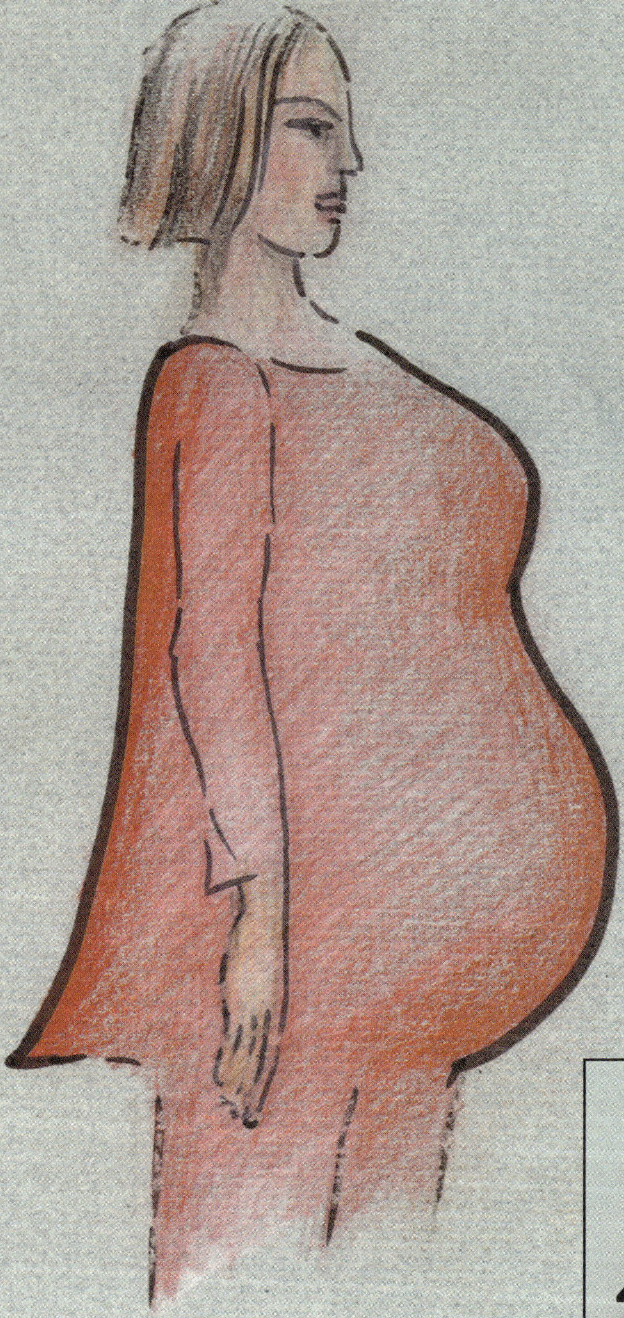

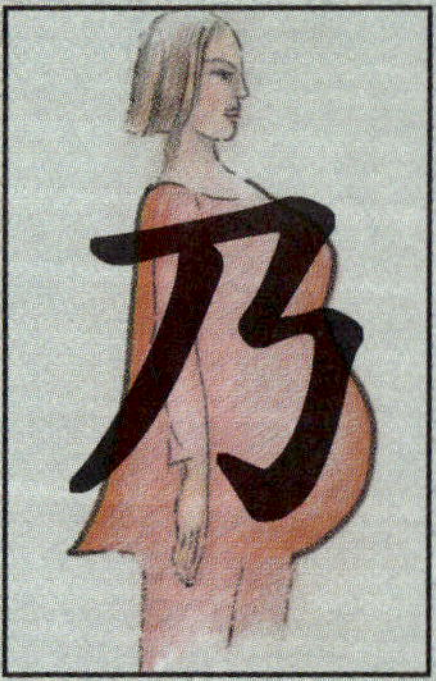

A pregnant women =乃[nǎi]= therefore; such.

乃

懷孕的女人 = 乃[nǎi] = 所以;因此

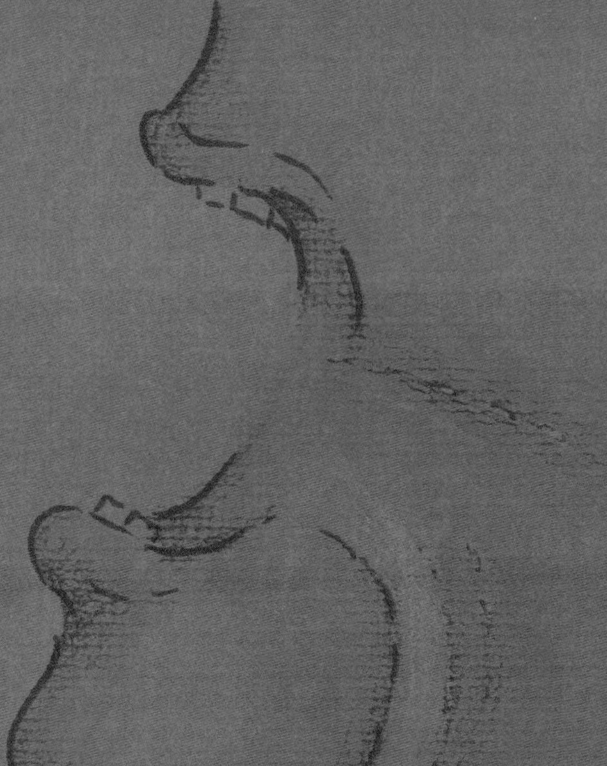

乞

An open mouth and passage of food to stomach
= 乞[qǐ] = to consume.

乞

丿 𠂉 乞

張開的嘴和食道 ＝ 乞[qǐ]＝ 張開嘴的

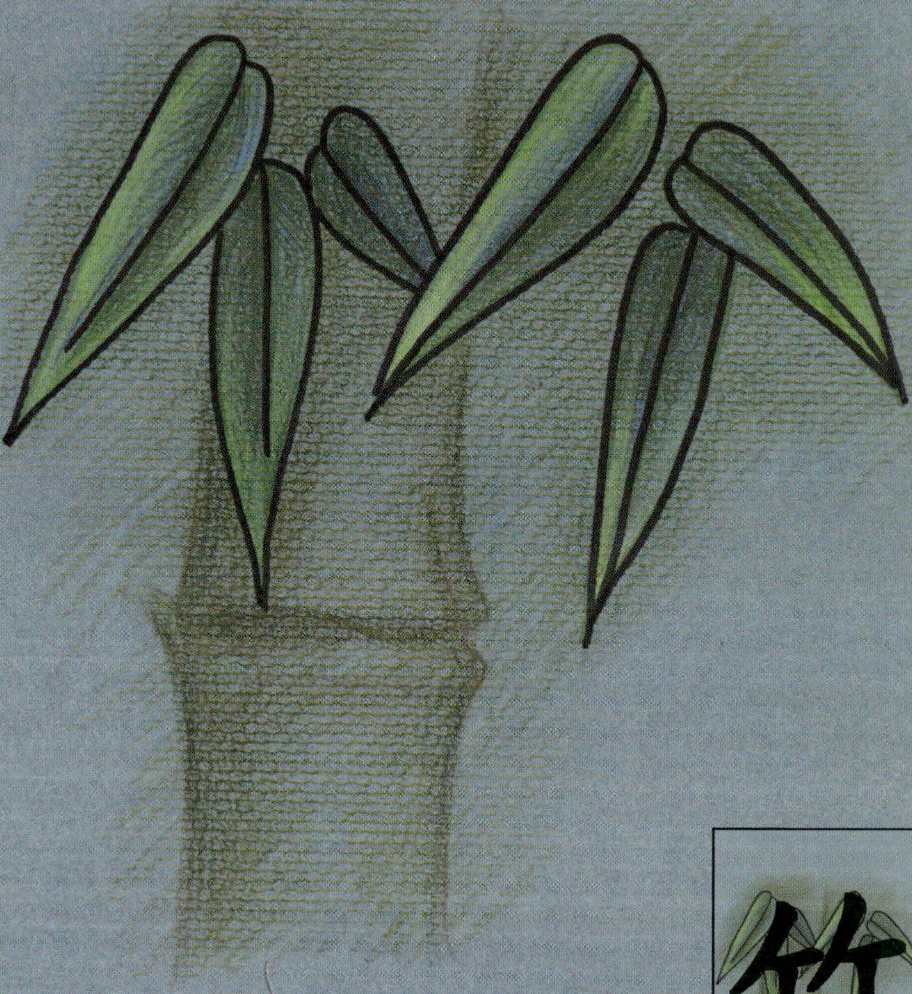

Two groups of three bamboo leaves = 竹[zhú] = bamboo.

竹

兩束三片的竹葉 = **竹**[zhú] = **竹子**

Head of a rice crop = 米 [mǐ] = rice, grain.

米

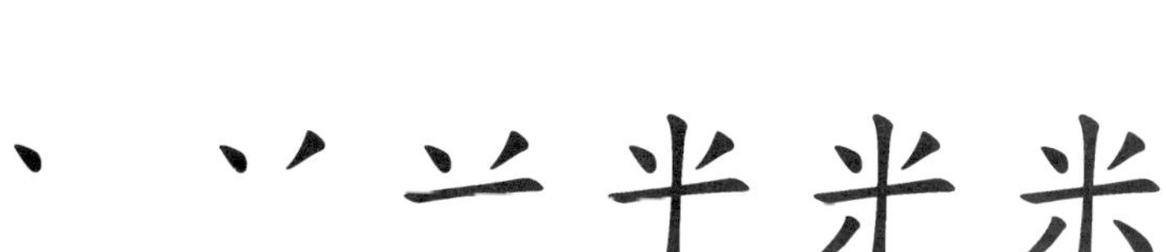

稻穗的頭端 = 米[mǐ] = **稻米;各種穀米**

A jar containing beans (plus lid) = 豆[dòu]= any type of bean.

豆

装豆子的罐子(和蓋子)＝ 豆[dòu]＝ 各種豆子

Other characters based on the characters shown in this book
用這本書裏介紹的字根造的字

1. 太[tài] = 'big' + an extra stroke = too, great (big with more added) /太=大 + 一點=比大還要多一點
2. 天[tiān] = 'big' + a top stroke = sky, heaven (the sky is bigger than the biggest man) /天=大 + 一橫=天空
3. 好[hǎo] = 'woman' + 'baby' = good; nice /好='女' + '子' =美好的
4. 安[ān] = 'roof' + 'woman' = peaceful /安= '宀' + '女' =平安
5. 字[zì] = 'roof' + 'baby' = words (babies learn their first words at home) /字= '宀' + '子' =文字(孩子通常在家裏學認字)
6. 姓[xìng] = 'woman' + 'birth' = surname (originally children took the mother's family name) /姓='女'+ '生' =姓(古時候中國人跟母親的姓)
7. 先[xiān] = 'scholar' + two legs + an extra stroke (tassel) = first (scholars usually walked ahead – i.e. first) /先= '士' + 兩條腿 + 一撇(髮簪的流蘇)=前先
8. 如[rú] = 'woman' + 'mouth' = if; as one wishes (in earlier years, a woman's words were considered as unreliable – suggesting uncertainty (if) – also, wishing is uncertain) /如= '女' + '口' =如果,如意(古時候人們認為女人說的話不可靠-所以有'如果'的意思.而且要能夠'如意'也不是一件可靠的事)
9. 吉[jí] = 'scholar' + 'mouth' = good luck (a scholar's words were considered to be good sense and leading to good fortune) /吉= '讀書人' + '口' =吉利(讀書人說的話應該是有道理而且會帶來好結果的)
10. 問[wèn] = 'door' + 'mouth' = ask (asking for information at someone's door) /問= '門' + '口' =問(迷路的人通常會到人家門口問路)
11. 們[mén] = 'person' + 'doors' (more than one door) = persons (more

than one person) /們=‘人’+‘門’(比一扇門多)=人們

12. 星[xīng] = ‘sun’ + ‘growing plant’ = star (a star can be seen through a growing plant /星=‘日’+‘生’=星星(可以從樹間看到)

13. 間[jiān] = ‘door’ + ‘sun’ (the sun seen between the entrance doors of a building) = between; the classifier for buildings / 間=‘門’+‘日’=中間;數建築物時用的單位詞

14. 閒[xián] = ‘door’ + ‘moon’ = to appreciate the moon through the gap of the door = leisure/閒=‘門’+‘月’=不是很重要的

15. 明[míng] = ‘sun’ + ‘moon’ = bright /明=‘日’+‘月’=明亮

16. 朋[péng] = ‘moon’ + ‘moon’ (two of the same kind coming together) = friend /朋=‘月’+‘月’=朋友

17. 多[duō] = two evening moons (normally only one)= many; much /多=兩個黃昏的月亮=不只一個

18. 名[míng] = ‘evening’ + ‘mouth’ = name (to be called in the dark evening)/名=‘夕’+‘口’=名字(是在夜晚看不清時用來叫人的)

19. 卡[qiǎ] = ‘up’ + ‘down’ = stuck /卡=‘上’+‘下’=不上不下,卡在中間

20. 串[chuàn] = a pole through two rings = to string together /串=一根木棍穿過兩個環形的中間=將東西連在一起

21. 少[shǎo] = ‘small’ with a stroke suggesting cutting = less /少=‘小’加上一撇表示減小一些=少

22. 少[shào] = juvenile /少=少年的

23. 妙[miào] = ‘woman’ + ‘juvenile’ = wonderful, interesting /妙=‘女’+‘少’=美好的，有趣的

24. 吵[chǎo] = ‘mouth’ + ‘juvenile’ = noise /吵=‘口’+‘少’=噪音

25. 尖[jiān] = ‘small’ upon ‘big’ = pointed shape, sharp /尖=‘小’在‘大’的上面=尖形,尖銳的

26. 洗[xǐ] = ‘water’ + ‘first’ = wash (to wash there must first be water) /洗=‘水’+‘先’=洗(要清洗必須先有水)

27. 沙[shā] = 'water' + 'less' = sand; finely crushed rock; soil that lacks of water /沙= '水' + '少' =很細的石粒;缺乏水份的土

28. 伙[huǒ] = 'person' + 'fire' = people utilise fire (cooking or keeping warm) /伙= '人' + '火' =人利用 火(煮飯或取暖)

29. 炒[chǎo] = 'fire' + 'less' = stir fry (needs less heat than deep fry) /炒 = '火' + '少' =炒(比炸用較小的火)

30. 炎[yén] = 'fire' + 'fire' = high heat /炎= '火+ '火' =高溫

31. 草[cǎo] = '早[zǎo](early)' (used for its sound) + '艹 (the radical for) grass' = (the modern version of) grass /草= '早' (用這個字的聲音) + '艹 (字根)' = (現在的寫法)草

32. 不[bù] = The 'below ground' part of the symbol for plant (there has been no growth yet) = no; not /不='木'字的下半部(植物還沒有長出來) =不是

33. 杯[bēi] = 'wood' + 'not' = cup (early cups were made from tree roots – the tree had to be removed first) /杯= '木' + '不' =杯(早期的杯子是由樹根做成-樹木已經先砍掉了)

34. 本[běn] = 'plant' + line suggesting its root, origin = root, origin, quantifier (for books as books were originally made from plants) /本 ='木' + 一橫來指出它的根部,來由=根本,來由,書本的單位詞(因為書本最先是用植物做成的)

35. 李[lǐ] = 'tree' + 'baby' = plum (the offspring of the tree) /李= '木' + '子' =李子(樹的子孫)

36. 呆[dāi] = 'mouth' + 'wood' = stupid /呆= '口' + '木' =不靈活的

37. 林[lín] = two plants = wood (a group of trees) /林=兩棵樹=樹林

38. 森[shēn] = three plants = forest /森=三棵樹=森林

39. 休[xiū] = 'man' + 'plant' = resting (under a tree – a big plant) /休= '人' + '木' = (人在大樹底下)休息

40. 棵[kē] = 'plant' + 'fruit' = unit is used to count plants /棵= '木' + '果' =計算植物所用的單位詞

41. 和 [hé] = 'crop' + 'mouth' = and, with, harmonious (a strong

connection – eventually became ‘and’ or ‘with’ and being close together – harmonious) /和=‘禾’ + ‘口’ =一起, 和諧(禾穀和嘴巴的關係密切和諧)

42. 秋[qīu] = ‘crop’ + ‘fire’ = autumn (stubble is burnt in autumn) /秋=‘禾’+‘火’=秋季(收割後燃燒殘株)

43. 男[nán] = ‘field’ + ‘strength’ = men (usually men worked in the fields) /男=‘田’+‘力’=男人(通常在田裏工作的是男人)

44. 奶[nǎi] = ‘woman’ + ‘pregnant woman’ = milk /奶=‘女’+‘乃’=奶水

45. 吃[chī] = ‘mouth’ + ‘consuming’ = eating /吃=‘口’ + ‘乞’ =張開嘴吃東西

Words made with characters shown in this book 用這本書裏介紹的字造的詞語

1. 大人[dà rén] = big person = adult
2. 大人們[dà rén mèn] = big persons = adults
3. 大間[dà jiān] = big building = large size (of houses)
4. 大門[dà mén] = big door = front door, gate
5. 太大[tài dà] = too big = too big
6. 太太[tài taì] = great great = Mrs., wife (of great importance in the family)
7. 女人[nǔ rén] = woman person = woman
8. 女生[nǔ shēng] = woman born = girl student, girl
9. 女士[nǔ shì] = woman scholar = lady
10. 女人間[nǔ rén jiān] = woman person between = between women
11. 好人[hǎo rén] = good person = good person
12. 好天[hǎo tiān] = good sky = good weather
13. 生字[shēng zì] = raw character = vocabulary
14. 先生[xiān shēng] = first born = Mr., husband (show respect for age)

15. 如果[rú guǒ] = if fruit = if (as fruit may not ripen, there is uncertainty)

16. 門口[mén kǒu] = door mouth = doorway, entrance

17. 開門[kāi mén] = open door = to open the door

18. 日子[rì zi] = sky baby = day

19. 生日[shēng rì] = birth day = birthday

20. 星星[xīng xīng] = star star = star

21. 閒人[xián rén] = leisure person = unauthorised person

22. 明天[míng tiān] = a bright day = tomorrow

23. 太早[tài zǎo] = too early = too early

24. 不早[bù zǎo] = not early = not early

25. 早上[zǎo shàng] = early up = morning

26. 早安[zǎo ān] = morning peaceful = good morning

27. 大多[dà duō] = big many = mostly

28. 太多[tài duō] = too many = too many, too much

29. 名字[míng zì] = name words = name

30. 名人[míng rén] = name person = well-known person

31. 天上[tiān shàng] = sky up = in the sky

32. 天下[tiān xià] = sky down = the world

33. 上午[shàng wǔ] = up noon = morning

34. 下午[xià wǔ] = down noon = afternoon

35. 中午[zhōng wǔ] = middle noon = midday

36. 中間[zhōng jiān] = middle in between = in the middle of

37. 串門子[chuàn mén zi] = string together doors = to visit friends' homes or gossip from door to door

38. 小人[xiǎo rén] = little man = mean person

39. 小子[xiǎo zi] = little child = kid

40. 太少[tài shǎo] = too less = insufficient

41. 少女[shào nǔ] = juvenile woman = young lady
42. 開水[kāi shǔi] = open water = boiled water
43. 開伙[kāi hǔo] = operation of utilising fire = to cook
44. 火星[hǔo xīng] = fire star = Mars
45. 水草[shǔi cǎo] = water grass = seagrass
46. 不大不小[bú dà bù xiǎo] = not big not small = just the right size
47. 不好[bù hǎo] = not good = not alright
48. 不多不少[bù dūo bù shǎo] = no more no less = just the right amount
49. 不妙[bú miào] = not wonderful = (matter) is not going well
50. 杯子[bēi zi] = cup baby = cup
51. 洗杯子[xǐ bēi zi] = wash cup = washing the cup
52. 本子[běn zi] = root baby = notebook
53. 本人[běn rén] = original person = oneself
54. 日本[rì běn] = sun origin = Japan
55. 李子[lǐ zi] = plum baby = plum fruit
56. 李先生[lǐ xiān shēng] = Mr. Li
57. 李太太[lǐ tài tai] = Mrs. Li
58. 呆子[dāi zi] = stupid baby = stupid person, idiot
59. 不呆[bù dāi] = not stupid = not stupid
60. 水果[shǔi gǔo] = water fruit = fruit
61. 小菜[xiǎo cài] = small vegetable = side dish
62. 炒菜[chǎo cài] = stir fry vegetable = stir fry dish, stir fry vegetable
63. 秋天[qīu tiān] = autumn day = autumn
64. 少年人[shào nían rén] = juvenile year person = young person
65. 中年人[zhōng nían rén] = middle year person = middle aged person
66. 去年[qù nían] = go year = last year
67. 來年[lái nían] = come year = the coming year, next year

68. 回去[húi qù] = return to go = leave

69. 菜田[cài tián] = vegetable field = vegetable field

70. 豆子[dòu zi] = bean = bean

71. 豆奶[dòu nǎi] = bean milk = soya bean milk

A list of English words with their Chinese characters illustrated in this book
這本書裏介紹的字和圖的頁碼索引